I0159408

CHUNKS
OF
GOODNESS

JILL THRUSSELL

CHUNKS OF GOODNESS

Copyright © 2019 Jill Thrussell
All rights reserved.
ISBN: 978-1-9999553-9-7

PREAMBLE

Inside this book of mysteries there is something
different to explore,
Because each verse considers life's ambiguities
that we so often may ignore,
Embark upon this adventure and step onto the
merry go ride,
When you open up the pages, you will discover
what lies inside,
Each page eagerly awaits your perusal be it day
or night,
So please enjoy the literary meander as curious
deliberations start to take flight,
You can rest your mind upon each sheet of
reflection, wisdom and advice,
And this blanket of comfort should warm your
heart when the world is as cold as ice.

CHUNKS OF GOODNESS

POETRY COLLECTION CONTENTS LIST

Inner Wealth:

Problems, Conflicts and Disappointments:

Life Choices and Emotional Survival Tools

Inner Wealth

CHUNKS OF GOODNESS

Hope and Sacrifice: A Heartbeat of Hope for Tomorrow

The arms of Hope were sad and heavy as she
began to cry,
But nothing could change the growing despair
inside her eyes,
Not an inch of hope existed that could save the
human child,
And so she had started to give up on her own
essence deep down inside.

Suddenly, a spark of light entered into the
hospital waiting room,
As Sacrifice rapidly started to arrive and not a
moment too soon,
With a familiar friendly face, open arms and a
hopeful smile,
He walked over to Hope and restored the chance of
another while.

You have done all you can now Hope, Sacrifice
said,
But I have come to assist you, so do not be afraid,
This child cannot be saved with only hope alone,
And a sacrifice must be given before he can return
home.

Inside that hopeless waiting room, a miracle was
suddenly sparked,

CHUNKS OF GOODNESS

As Sacrifice began his work and found a
replacement heart,
A donor was quickly found to save the male child's
human life,
And so Hope could finally smile again as Sacrifice
solved her strife.
Another chance would now be given for a young
man to live,
Because Hope and Sacrifice had given him all that
they could give,
So in a moment filled with heartbreak and despair
that day, Hope had swiftly learned,
That Sacrifice really was her true companion and
truly her best friend.

Hope turned to Sacrifice and smiled as they
began to depart,
And thanked him for his provision, the sacrifice of a
human heart,
Without you I couldn't have saved him, Hope rapidly
confessed,
Without the sacrifice that you found that young man
would now be dead.

Hope, take my hand and walk with me, Sacrifice
implored,
You will never be alone and your efforts won't be
ignored,
Alone you cannot achieve as much and I am here for
you,

CHUNKS OF GOODNESS

Because together we can move mountains and change what is true.

Lady Trust

In a golden dress she walks softly through the
centre of your heart,
And every day is peaceful as she plays her silent
part,
She wears her heart of trust upon her golden
sleeve,
As she encourages you to put faith in those you
trust in and believe.

A fragile silent strength that cannot ever be seen,
She visits you each day and night silently like a
quiet dream,
Beauty, honour and respect form every part of
her name,
And dignity adorns every single inch of her frame.

But when the monsters of lies and deceit
suddenly draw near,
Lady Trust will run away as she starts to hide in
fear,
Because every arrow they fire towards her will
shatter her pure truth,
Into a million pieces and she has to preserve her
youth.

They say that when she leaves a bond that she
will not return,
As the relationship turns sours and logs of hurt

swiftly start to burn,
Sometimes she may try to return but she will
never be the same,
Because the ruins of trust are hard to rebuild
from the debris of disappointed pain.

Happiness is a Present

Happiness is a present that we must give to
ourselves as often as can,
Because tomorrow is not guaranteed and it can
slip so quickly from our hands,
No warranties are ever provided for human
mortal lives,
And there is no repair technician available to fix
any of our human strife.

An abundant package of joy from oneself can
dispel any tearful heartbreak and miserable rain,
And usher in rays of sunshine to dismiss any
distress, discomfort and pain,
At times there is nobody else nearby to deliver
that gift directly to our hearts,
And so, we must give ourselves that gift regularly
to maintain our lives, so that we do not fall apart.

Battlefield of Emotions

Inside the kingdom of your mind, body and heart,
There are several daily battles, of which you are a part,
And although reason and logic are sharper than swords,
Emotions can overrule them with just a few words.

In every single corner of your heart, body and mind,
There are many different fights that you may stumble across and find,
Because not a second of the day passes by that you do not think, feel or live,
But who wins each battle daily is a victory that only you can give.

If Sadness and Anger prepare to battle and then start to fight,
They can battle all day and well into the night,
Once they have finished their deadly, ugly hard clash,
Your body can feel so drained and be in a total mish mash.

If Joy and Envy conflict and then begin to duel,
That is when you will learn that Joy really is your best tool,

CHUNKS OF GOODNESS

The battle may continue all through the day,
But eventually Joy will finally take Envy's scorn
away.

If Fear shows up willing and ready for a scrap,
Then Bravery and Courage will need to make a
start,
Once they team up together, Fear will rapidly
begin to flee,
Because Fear cannot stand strength that he
cannot see.

If Hope and Vengeance decide to suddenly lock
horns,
Life will not be simple as Vengeance taunts and
scorns,
The battle will not be easy because Vengeance is
oh so strong,
But finally Hope will overcome Vengeance's
wrongs.

If Logic and Reason decide that they wish to
enter and then they jump in,
The battle will become even more complex as
those two begin,
A struggle may ensue that has no quick end,
But finally, you will discover that Reason really is
your best friend.

At the end of each daily battle the truth will start

CHUNKS OF GOODNESS

to become so clear,
That your emotions can be your strongest
weapons but can also form your biggest fears,
However, when Reason and Logic decide once
more to fully occupy their thrones,
Your emotional foot soldiers will bow down to
them and then return to their homes.

Emotional Destinations: Joy, Sorrow, Surprise and Fear

Inside our minds there are many different places
that we can reside in and live,
Which our emotional experiences shape, evoke,
enable, foster and give,
At least eight possible destinations exist that we
can visit every day,
As we meander through the course of our lives
and try to find our way.

The Mountains of Joy are really a great place to
see and be,
Because happiness can lift your mind up high and
set your worries free,
Every minute that you spend there will be a truly
pleasant affair,
Because joy is a delightful destination with an
imaginative flair.

When you decide to visit to the angry, turbulent,
rocky Bay of Wrath,
On that day you will abhor everything and
everyone that dares to cross your path,
Like a chaotic storm, angry rage will swirl around
inside your mind,
And not an ounce of joy or peace will you be able
to find.

CHUNKS OF GOODNESS

If you manage to pay a visit to the magnificent,
sparkly Tower of Trust,
Your day will be filled with sacks of kindness and
full of bags of love,
Because when Devotion and Affection approach
you and take you by the hand,
They will guide you into a warm, friendly,
peaceful place and a beautiful land.

The Lake of Sorrow unfortunately, can be tragic,
murky and oh so very deep,
And if you wade into its depths, the waves may
engulf you and you may even start to weep,
Once you are surrounded by drops of sadness,
waves of gloom and tides of despair,
Your broken heart may become saturated by
sadness which will then be difficult to repair.

A beautiful place you must try to visit regularly is
the Skyscraper of Surprise,
Because it can make your heart flutter with
absolute delight and astonish your eyes,
Every wonder can be viewed from its amazingly
tall, very high heights,
And spectacular astounding visions will start to
occupy some of your days and nights.

Deep inside the terrible, horrible, scary dense
Forest of Fear,
You will find no warmth or comfort and

CHUNKS OF GOODNESS

absolutely nothing sincere,
And as each clump of twisted, tangled wood
surrounds your inner form,
Creatures may lurk behind each tree that might
pounce upon you like a savage swarm.

Inside the Ark of Anticipation life can be a very
mixed and jumbled bag,
Because optimism can make you happy but
pessimism make you feel so sad,
Joyful Hope may come and welcome you, take
your hand and lead you inside,
But try to avoid grumpy Cynicism's company
because a smile he will not provide.

A tour of the Disgusting Dimension can really be
quite rare,
But if you decide to pay it a visit, of one thing you
must always be aware,
Disgust can be an uncomfortable place to visit,
live in or reside,
Because from your scowl, disdain and discomfort,
everyone around you will try to hide.

So, when you start to embark upon the voyage of
your new day,
Choose your destinations wisely and where you
would really like to stay,
Because each place that you can visit will offer a
very different type of mood,

CHUNKS OF GOODNESS

So, try to choose an enjoyable place to spend your day that will make you feel really good.

The Wardrobe of My Mind

On Monday I dressed in confidence with her
glamour and flair,
The day was bright and wonderful as she lifted
me high up in the air,
Every step throughout that day truly was a
pleasure to be had,
Because she gave me the courage to be happy
and not sad.

On Tuesday I wore anger with his deadly, vicious
stare,
Someone had upset me and the day was a
nightmare,
Every minute was very ugly because an angry
cloud hung over my head,
But finally, relief came at night when I went to
bed.

On Wednesday I gave forgiveness the chance to
adorn my frame,
As love took my hand and guided me onto that
peaceful train,
Sometimes the ride was difficult but it was worth
the pain,
Because by the end of the evening, I could finally
smile again.

On Thursday I picked a suit of hope and my life

was not the same,
Because pleasant expectations joyfully filled and
occupied my brain,
Everything around me was truly a pleasure to be
heard and seen,
As I chose to fill my mind, heart and life with
hopes from a dream.

On Friday I clothed myself in happiness as I
prepared for the weekend,
The week had been so very long and the
weekend is my best friend,
Another week will definitely start again, oh so
very soon,
But this time I will prepare the wardrobe of my
mind and give my thoughts a fine tune.

Clothes of Confidence

Inside my mind there is a very special piece of
attire that I sometimes wear,
Which I save for rainy days that might potentially
be gloomy and lack any joyful flair,
This very special outfit has been formed and cut
from the material thoughts of hope,
And it is held together by the threads of
anticipation which provide even greater scope.

Formed from hopeful material and sewn together
by a needle of encouragement that shines so bright,
This outfit can only be seen internally by me and
not by any other human being's eyesight,
When my day ahead looks dreary, I clothe my
thoughts in this optimistic outfit,
And it motivates and strengthens me, so that I
can face the hurdles of life with a hopeful spirit.

Confidence can restore hope inside our hearts
when the path of life looks very sad and dim,
And confidence can revive our dignity when our
lives have been crushed and we feel downtrodden,
Our confidence is a celebration of who we are
and what we hope we can achieve,
That revitalizes our spirit and assists us as it helps
us to realize any plans that we may conceive.

Sometimes there is no pillar of strength to be our

encouragement, support and stable rock,
So, an outfit of confidence is required to clothe
and lift our minds when we receive a painful knock,
The blows from rejection on our walk-through life
can at times, knock us completely of our feet,
And the ropes of disappointment can bind our
hearts to the ground and make us feel so weak.

Whenever the world around me disappoints and
defeats me, or just seems so very bleak,
Then I reach into the wardrobe of my mind and
my clothes of confidence I do fervently seek,
The invisible clothes that I wear inside my
thoughts that no one else can see, feel or touch,
Somehow can then always restore my heart and
smile as hopeful encouragement starts to fill me up.

Treasure Chest of Memories

Every day that the morning greets me another
opportunity arrives,
To create some joyful memories that might
comfort me inside,
Some memories that I make might be very
pleasant and some I may choose not to store,
But I will pack those that I wish to keep inside my
treasure chest whilst others I will ignore.

The treasure chest of memories that lives inside
my heart and mind,
Has several different storage bays filled with
memories of several different kinds,
Some memories are formed from experiences
with others of moments that we shared,
As they pay homage to the people that played a
part in my life and those who truly cared.

Memories purely formed from jewels of joy,
reside in a very special place,
Because when I recall those past moments inside
my mind, each one brings a joyful smile to my face,
Those memories are highly treasured because
they cannot be repeated or replaced,
But new jewels of joy can be added to that pile as
each day is lived out and embraced.

Teardrops of sadness form some memories inside

that chest that can make me feel so forlorn and sad,
But I really have to keep each one because they
remind me to appreciate life and to be glad,
When I explore some of those sad memories,
they can bring tears to my eyes,
Yet I cannot live without those precious, sad
moments, a truth I fully recognize.

Some memories are kept to guide me and to
steer me through the landscape of my life,
Because they teach me valuable lessons and a
source of wisdom they provide,
Some memories are my companion and offer me
a form of friendship when I am on my own,
Because when I reminisce upon pleasant times
that I spent with those I love, I am never truly alone.

Other memories form a source of hope of to me
and ignite my dreams to be realized,
And at times, some can even shield me from rainy
days and bring sunshine to the skies,
Every spark of joyful hope from the past can
nurture and fertilize my life, thoughts and plans,
And so those memories are invaluable to me
because each one can bring and provide wisdom to
my hands.

But inside one of the storage bays live some
memories of a truly different sort and kind,
The memories formed from the prickly thorns of

pain which can never be forgotten or left behind,
Each one provides a painful reminder of things
that I should not participate in, say or do,
As they warn of all kinds of danger that can visit
me and of people that are untrue.

Each memory that lives inside my treasure chest
has a different reason to be preserved,
So, from the jewels of joy and teardrops of
sadness to the thorns of pain, I store each one
undeterred,
Some memories can provide guidance, wisdom
and experience, so that I am not easily led astray,
And although some may be ugly and are truly
hard, each one teaches me lessons about life every
day.

Value Added You

A product sits upon the shelf of life that people
might wish to buy into,
But that product is not a manufactured good and
that product is actually, really you,
Each one of us has an intrinsic desire to be loved,
wanted and to belong,
But if our package of existence does not appeal
to anyone that we like, it can be hard to get along.

The first thing that we must consider is if we
would actually buy into ourselves,
Because time and emotions are an investment
that we give to those that we pick out from life's
shelf,
Every minute that we spend with someone we
choose is an allocation of our time,
As we commit to them and build a relationship
that is more personal and individually refined.

Just like any product, our human product,
packaging and life-cycle can always be improved,
If we take steps to invest in ourselves with time,
resources, care and nutritious food,
Value can be added daily in so many ways to our
minds, bodies, lifestyles and hearts,
If we choose to spend our time constructively and
with negativity we try to part.

CHUNKS OF GOODNESS

Our personal physical presentation is our
packaging, much like the icing on a cake,
But we must package ourselves in a way that is
true to who we are, make no mistake,
False advertising can be misleading and create
expectations that will not ever be realized,
But if we align our exteriors with our internal
character, our packaging will never be a disguise.

Underneath the surface of our external packaging
there sits our personalities, characters and attributes,
And as we present ourselves to those who choose
to spend time with us, our qualities they may start to
peruse,
Each shared moment and experience are an
investment that all parties involved have to make,
Because each lived out moment that we spend
with someone, means other choices we chose to
forsake.

Our relationships with others can add another
layer of value to our daily lives,
If we choose our friends, lovers and associates
wisely and try to avoid any negative strife,
One thing you must always remember however,
as you select those that you feel are worthy of your
time,
If they do not truly appreciate you, your
emotional investment in them will not be worth a
dime.

CHUNKS OF GOODNESS

A Value-Added Life, you must always try to bear
in mind is not just a one-way street,
Because you can also add value to those that
cross your path whenever you decide to meet,
Encouragement, support and advice will not cost
you a single material thing,
And a bag of positivity is definitely something
that to any relationship you can always bring.

Gifts of Life, Love and Heartbreak: Portions of Desire and Glasses of Comfort

When life offers us the gift of existence every
morning and we have a chance to enjoy each new
day,
Then we can joyfully unwrap that gift as we
venture down our chosen paths and go along our
way,
Other gifts we may find and choose upon our
walk as we wander through each minute that passes
by,
And some of those gifts may contain jewels of joy
that can bring rays of sunshine to our skies,
Some other gifts are different and contain
teardrops of sadness due to events that cause upset,
But each gift is invaluable because they can teach
us about love, compassion, decency and respect.

Although the terrain of life may be rocky and the
mountains of obstruction oh so very high,
Obstacles and hurdles can teach us to be diligent
and that is a lesson that money cannot ever buy,
Love may decide to bless our lives and that
wonderful gift can be so very unique and rare,
As we learn to appreciate our family, romances
and friendships and every shoulder of supportive
care,
Heartbreak on the other hand can be rocky and

treacherous with pain that cuts our hearts and minds
so deep,
Because the sides of the valley of misery that
heartbreak resides within can be very steep.

During our daily adventures, we may choose to
indulge in some portions of desire,
As we seek to satisfy any passionate urges that
reside within us which can spark and ignite a warm,
joyful fire,
But sometimes we may be brought abruptly back
down to Earth with a rocky, sudden bump,
Because some portions of desire may contain
hidden, indigestible, inedible, very bitter lumps,
If one day our dreams are shattered and our
hearts end up crushed and trampled into the
ground,
That is when a soothing glass of comfort and hug
of love must then be sought and found.

Life is not always pleasant and some of our
dreams may not actually come true,
But every morning that we wake up is a gift to
appreciate as each day our life is renewed,
One day we may look back upon our lives and
perhaps wish that we had done so much more,
As our spirit is called back to its home and starts
to leave our human mortal core,
So, there is one thing that we must remember as
the daily gifts of life, love and heartbreak are given

CHUNKS OF GOODNESS

to our hearts,
We only have one life to live and appreciate, so
we must try to find joy in every part.

Problems, Conflicts and Disappointments:

1. Ghosts and Shadows
2. Promises
3. Prison of False Hope
4. The Bitter Pills of Regret
5. Slumber of Lies
6. Trophies of Pain
7. Remnants of Yesterday
8. The Best Mistake You Will Ever Make
9. Shields of Truth and Love
10. Eviction from My Heart

Ghosts and Shadows

Where can we go and hide, what can we try to
do,
When the ghosts and shadows from our life start
to pursue,
What do they want from us, we may start to
question and ask,
Why won't they leave us alone and what are their
fearful objectives and tasks.

At night they may attack us from inside our
nightmares,
As their ghostly, dark forms catch us fast asleep,
unprepared and unaware,
An answer to the many questions that we may
never have a chance to ask,
At first will perhaps elude us as we seek a
connection to our present or our past.

If we seek a remedy to the unknown ghosts that
haunt our nights and days,
It can lead us on a wild goose chase and then we
may start to lose our way,
But in some respects, there may be a solution to
some of the shadows from the past,
Because if they can be faced and any differences
reconciled, then peace may finally be made at last.

Promises

Inside of us there is a hidden land which nobody
else really sees or knows,
And that is the land where promises live once
they have been given and composed,
Once a promise has been ignited it exists deep
inside our minds and hearts,
And each one starts to live and breathe within us
as we wait for them to materialize and start.

The promises that we give at times to others can
be a very complex bunch,
Because if we do not fulfil them, upon our heads
our own words start to crunch,
A promise that we make to someone else is a
debt which must then be satisfied,
Or from the people that placed their trust in us,
we may have to hide.

A promise that is given to us can be a joyful
delight to our ears,
But if we have to wait too long for it to manifest
in reality that may spark some inner fears,
What we must always try to remember is that
some people are really not sincere,
And that their false promises are meaningless
because to their lies, truth is nowhere near.

Prison of False Hope

You told me a lie that I innocently believed,
And so, your prison of false hope was rapidly
conceived,
Each lie of false hope formed a cast iron bar,
That entrapped and ensnared me from near and
afar,
Every day then became a wait of tedious misery,
As I waited for your promises that would never
ever be.

The first prison bar you used to tie me up in
hopeful, wishful knots,
Was the lie of true love which tantalized my
thoughts,
But I learnt very quickly when I gave you the
romantic chance,
Your love was nothing but a lie, devoid of any
joyful romance,
Fakeness not commitment, I realized, is your
specialty,
Because your lie of devotion rapidly became
apparent to see.

The second prison bar that you used to trap and
ensnare me,
Was the promise of a very special economic
opportunity,
But just like your lying lips and your false tongue,

CHUNKS OF GOODNESS

Once again, a real manifestation did not seem to
come,
As the truth drew closer to me and your lies
disappeared,
Another prison bar of false hope was finally
revealed.

The third and final prison bar you utilized
deceptively,
Wrapped itself around my future like a golden
possibility,
That final lie you verbalized from deep inside
your mind,
Was a seductive enticement of a material
financial kind,
You uttered your daily lies of false hope to me
with so much pride,
But now I have grown wise enough to step of
your fake merry-go-ride.

Dirty truths lay hidden deep inside your thoughts,
That you clothe with words of sweetness which
only result in noughts,
Disappointment and heartbreak sadly became
very good friends of mine,
Because you introduced me to them every single
time,
But now finally from your prison of fakeness,
deception and lies,
I can walk freely from the false promises that you

CHUNKS OF GOODNESS

disguise.

The Bitter Pills of Regret

Upon the shelves inside my mind there are some
very bitter pills to be found,
Which present themselves now and again,
despite life's joyful nature and its pleasant sounds,
Each one can have a sour, bitter taste that ushers
in sadness, pain and frets,
Because the hardest pills in life to swallow are the
bitter pills of regret.

Disappointment when consumed always has a
very sour after-taste,
Because how other people let us down is not
something that we like to face,
Sometimes they may have crushed our hopes and
dreams without a single care,
But people's promises are not always true and of
that we must always be aware.

Heartbreak sits all alone upon a very solemn,
painful shelf,
Over what somebody else did to us and what we
did to ourselves,
A broken heart is never truly soothed by that
bitter pill of pain,
No matter how many times in life people may try
to explain.

Loss is not something in life that we can ever

CHUNKS OF GOODNESS

really control,
And when we lose someone that we love, it
deeply grieves our soul,
Regrets can flurry through our minds like a
speeding train,
Of things we should have said and done but now
cannot partake in again.

Wrongs we have done to someone else can fester
inside our minds,
Because when they confronted us, there was
nowhere for us to hide,
Guilt can weigh our bodies down and as we try to
carry that weight,
That bitter pill is no easier to consume and it can
cause our throats to grate.

Mistakes that we have made are like ghosts from
the past which can haunt us every night,
When we consider the things, we should have
done differently and what we did not do right,
But our actions from the past can never be
reversed, changed or undone,
Because time is not at our convenience to play
with just for fun.

For the many bitter pills of regret there really is
only one actual cure,
Because to swallow them every day is not a life
that we would want to endure,

CHUNKS OF GOODNESS

A bottle of sweet honey sits upon another shelf
of that we can be sure,
But to drink it means that we must face our past
to find closure and try to mature.

Sometimes forgiveness is a gift that we have to
give to ourselves,
Because mistakes and wrongs that we have
already committed cannot be reversed,
Sometimes we must make up for the
disappointments that we received,
Because time waits for nobody and nothing, no
matter how much our hearts grieve.

So, do not wait until you lose someone to love
them every day,
Because tomorrow is not promised and you can
still love them today,
Do not give your heart to someone that with your
emotions will play,
Because you are worth more than that in every
single way.

Slumber of Lies

The blanket of lies that temporarily kept me
warm,
Provided me with shelter during a very harsh
storm,
But all the warning signs I did mistakenly ignore,
Until a bolt of truth awoke me and I could
slumber no more,
Like a lightning shot that struck me straight from
the skies,
The truth pierced my mind and suddenly
obliterated all the lies,
So now, I am fully awake and my thoughts are full
of regret,
But there are no seeds of comfort just worried
beads of sweat.

A ton of lies had coiled around my life like a silent
snake,
As I had slept through the dream of deceit and
from it I did not awake,
But now as the lightning of truth strikes me, I
start to realize,
To sleep in the false comfort of falsehood, truly is
not wise,
The temporary invisible warmth that lies can
secretly and discreetly provide,
Can appease your heart momentarily as you sit
upon a fake merry-go-ride,

But when the truth finally returns and starts to
strike your core,
Suddenly, the merry-go-ride of falsehood will
come to a twisted, bitter end once more.

Now inside my mind I have built a golden throne
for the Truth,
As I seek to preserve the jewelled crown of purity
that adorns her youth,
And although Truth can seem far colder, you
really cannot sit upon the fence,
Because if you embrace Truth willingly, your joy
will never be a pretence,
And though there may be some sadness and
there may even be some painful tears,
Truth will find a way to comfort you as she guides
you through the years,
When Truth rules your heart and mind, she will be
kind, courteous and fair,
But if you allow Deceit to keep your heart warm,
he will only drag you down into a pit of despair.

Trophies of Pain

Upon the shelf of bravery deep inside my mind,
There are several trophies of pain that I can easily
find,
Each one carries an emotional scar that so deeply
hurts,
From the times I trusted, loved and lived just a
little bit too much.

Every single hurtful risk I took was a very painful
step,
And so, upon each unpleasant lesson I can
silently reflect,
Nothing it seems can prepare you for the various
trials of life,
But my trophies of pain ensure that I remember
the injuries that cut through my heart like a knife.

The first golden trophy that stands upon the
shelf, so very tall and proud,
Came from a romantic heartbreak that beat my
heart into the ground,
I willingly gave my heart to someone that I
adored and loved,
But their area of expertise was pain and so my
heart was truly crushed.

Further along the shelf of bravery a modest silver
trophy stands,

CHUNKS OF GOODNESS

But that trophy was sadly gained from placing
trust in the wrong hands,
I was guided into paths of danger, treachery and
surrounded by fear,
As I was led into a jungle of betrayal that brought
only sorrow and tears.

One final bronze trophy sits quietly upon that
bravery shelf,
That relates to a mistake that I made when I was
truly not myself,
Wisdom had abandoned me as I was suddenly
tempted and led astray,
And as my mind indulged in destructive
temptations, I sadly lost my way.

Each trophy that sits upon that shelf silently
reminds me every single day,
Of how I endured and overcame life's trials on my
solitary way,
Every painful scar is engraved deep inside my
thoughts and heart,
But those scars are not the end of my life, they
are merely just the start.

A positive future awaits me on the horizon of my
dreams,
Because the past that stands behind me like a
shadow is not always what it seems,
A new day can give me another chance to live,

CHUNKS OF GOODNESS

And another day can give my broken heart a
chance to forgive.

Remnants of Yesterday

Every morning when I wake up the first thing that
I must do,
Is remove all the cobwebs that have gathered like
drops of dew,
Inside the passageways of my mind there is a
garbage bag,
Which I can fill with any unwanted remnants of
yesterday that will make me truly sad,
But as I start to brush up all the painful debris of
what happened yesterday,
I carefully consider each one before I attempt to
put those painful cobwebs away,
Because there are lessons that I must learn and
nuggets of wisdom that I must gain,
Which are thoughtfully reviewed before being
processed by my brain,
Because before I can face the coming challenges
and hurdles of today,
I must listen to the messages from life that
yesterday's journey has to say.

The Best Mistake You Will Ever Make

One lesson throughout my life that I have truly
learned,
Is that not every mistake I meet upon my path
will actually be my friend,
Some mistakes can destroy your life, crush your
heart and tear you down,
And burden your life with sadness, tears and a
very heavy frown,
But amongst all the ugly mistakes you make in
life you might find a rare jewel of hope,
Because some mistakes can be a blessing and
provide us with an actual lifeboat.

When Honest Mistake is met upon our paths, she
can teach us the right way,
And provide us with a chance to correct the
things that we think, do or say,
Although we may face large hurdles, tearful
regrets and elements of surprise,
A meeting with Honest Mistake can ultimately,
truly be a blessing in disguise.
Because at the end of a struggle with hearty,
positive Honest Mistake,
We can learn from our misstep what changes we
must make.

Negative Mistake can be the worst enemy to ever

cross our paths,
Because he leaves a permanent scar from our
folly as he scorns and laughs,
Our downfall may be immediate, or it could even
take many years,
As our mistake becomes a clifftop that we will fall
from, formed from our errors and fears,
If a clash with Negative Mistake is so severe that
he stands upon our heads,
We may even start to hate our own lives and wish
that we were dead.

The best mistake to meet in life is Positive
Mistake since he will change your ways,
Because that mistake will teach you how to live
your life in a way that people praise,
Although his correction may come with heavy
responsibilities and even lots of stress,
If you meet Positive Mistake upon your path, it is
always truly for the best,
Once you have endured the pain that your error
caused and all the lessons have been learnt,
Your life will then change positively because your
medal of bravery you will have fully earnt.

Shields of Truth and Love

If you adorn your inner self with the shields of
truth and love which are very strong,
They can protect you from the harsh attacks and
shadows of those that may wish to do you wrong,
If their vicious, savage claws suddenly dig into
you when your enemies start to pounce,
The shields of truth and love can then be utilized
to eradicate every harmful ounce,
Jagged lies and hurtful attacks from evil doers
may threaten to destroy every part of you inside,
But protection can be found behind the shields of
truth and love which provide a safe place for you to
hide,
Venomous arrows of hatred may fly towards you
and fill your heart with absolute despair,
And although you can seek shelter from attacks
behind your shields you must always try to be aware,
Not everyone that you meet in life will like you
and will want to be your friend,
And some people will really despise you although
they might smile in your face and try to pretend,
A shield of truth can protect you from the things
that they may say or do to you,
And a shield of love can provide comfort from
the misery that they may want to put you through.

Eviction from My Heart

The love that you promised me was not actually
real or true,
So now there is only one thing that I can very
sadly do,
Because a year has gone by but you are still the
same,
And only heartbreak and betrayal form every part
of your name.

Every day that I have allowed you to occupy a
space deep inside my heart,
You have trampled on my good intentions and
torn my heart apart,
So now, I am crushed and broken, disappointed
and full of despair,
Because our love is not something that my love
for you can ever repair.

An eviction order must be issued now to evict
you from my heart and life,
Because my life is too short to spend it buried in
your strife,
Somewhere else another house of love waits for
me where I can happily reside,
That will offer me a mansion not a filthy
basement, decorated in the betrayal that you cannot
hide.

CHUNKS OF GOODNESS

Some bitter taunts of romantic failure remain that
still occupy and haunt my mind,
But I can no longer tolerate the second-class love
that you provide,
Somewhere out there in this world, someone else
may care for me,
In a way that is truly beautiful and sincere and
that reality I now see.

Blinded by my love and passion for you which
was sadly not returned,
My heart was absolutely crushed, torn apart,
shattered and spurned,
So now, there is only one thing I can do as from
your house of misery I depart,
An eviction notice must be issued to ban you
from my life and broken heart.

Obstacles of Life and Hurdles of the Heart:

Our Teacher of the Past, Companion of the Present and Our Future Unborn Child of Hope

When yesterday came to visit me and knocked
upon my door,
The loud tap Past gave, I could not ignore,
Come with me, Past said, and do not be afraid,
I have a lesson to teach you and you must be
very brave,
And as I walked along with him through the
history my life,
Nerves leapt around inside of me as I reviewed
my moments of painful strife,
Past began to discuss my mistakes with me as he
pointed each one out,
You must make corrections, Past advised, of that
there really is no doubt,
Mistakes are not the end of you because you
have a chance to change,
And life can be different, if you make restitution
and try to rearrange,
Your thoughts, actions and attitude which can
make or break you,
Because the Past is always behind you that much
is very true,
Past rapidly began to discuss with me the path
that I should take,
Whilst I tried to understand my history and every

single mistake,
He advised me of my faults and errors that
seemed so very wrong,
But encouraged me to learn from each of them
and then try to carry on.

When Present discovered that I had just met with
the Past,
She began to smile as she acknowledged that he
was very fast,
I will take your hand and guide you now through
the current storm,
She encouraged as she took my hand and
advised me to hold on,
I can walk with you through this day and help you
to see,
The life you that should try to live and all the
things that you should be,
Life is not always easy and the path is not always
straight,
But life can be improved so much if you try to
embrace your fate,
Every day is a chance to change and to fix your
past regrets,
If you embrace me the Present and try to face the
world with honour and respect,
Our morning has just begun and I can lead you
through this day,
But you really must take heed of everything that
Past had to say,

CHUNKS OF GOODNESS

I will never abandon you or leave your side
because I am always here,
Present reassured me as for our day she began to
prepare,
That day sped by so rapidly but Present kept me
strong,
Because her faithful hands held onto me lovingly
so that I could carry on.

When the night finally arrived and as I lay down
inside my bed,
The Future came to visit me as dreams quickly
began to fill up my head,
I am the unborn child of hope, Future told me,
And I bring all the possibilities of what your life
could truly be,
That night as Future played with me, we danced
to a pleasant tune,
And I embraced each vision of hope as I wished
that each one would happen soon,
Every vision that Future brought to me was filled
with so much joy,
And so the night quickly slipped by in almost the
blink of an eye,
When the morning showed up, Future whispered
to me as he prepared to leave,
I'll leave you now but dreams can come true and
that I truly believe,
Each unborn hope and dream I'd had that night

then rapidly did depart,
But once my eyes were wide open, Present
quickly began to make a start,
She gently took my hand again as we watched
Future disappear,
I am here to guide you through this day, Present
said, because Future is no longer here,
Present started to advise me with words of
wisdom as she led the way,
Tomorrow cannot possibly arrive my dear, until
you have lived today.

The Blanket of Dreams and the Dagger of Reality

The battle began suddenly when the Dagger of
Reality turned up to fight,
With the soft Blanket of Dreams that kept me
warm each and every night,
Dagger of Reality was formed from a hard, sharp
blade of steel,
And every part of Dreams was rapidly cut away as
the hard truths Reality did reveal,
Being that Blanket of Dreams is gentle, soft and
extremely kind,
Dreams was no match for Reality, I rapidly did
find,
Every slash from Reality's blade ruthlessly cut
away at every single hope,
As my dreams began to slide quickly down
Reality's slippery slope,
When the battle finally came to an end and as I
began to awake,
Dreams I noticed had already fled and hidden for
survival's sake,
Another night would definitely return to my life
later on that day,
And so, I remained hopeful that Dreams would
also return and that my future hopes had not been
scared away.

Opportunities: Friends or Foes?

A sunny morning arrived and as I joyfully greeted
the new day,
Onto the path of my life a random Golden
Opportunity did stray,
Upon his face there was a cheery, hearty, warm,
friendly smile,
As Golden Opportunity walked alongside me and we
chatted for a while.

Hopeful enthusiasm and eager anticipation, rapidly
began to fill my mind,
As Golden Opportunity explained to me the chance
that he wanted to provide,
A part of me was excited and wanted to dive straight
into the deep end,
But hesitation suddenly gripped me as I considered
that this Golden Opportunity might not be an actual
friend.

An opportunity can change your life and help you to
realize your dreams,
But it could also destroy you and rip your life apart
at the seams,
Not every opportunity that crosses your path is
offered for positive ends,
Because some are formed from hatred and laced
with destructive pretense.

Doors of Access: Relationships and Opportunities

Each day in life we are surrounded by many invisible
access doors,
And there are mainly two types of doors which can
be more fully explored,
Some doors provide access to relationships and
other doors access to opportunities,
And both can provide us with the potential to live
our lives successfully and happily.

Doors of access when opened can allow others into
our personal space,
And so, those doors that we control can be opened
up at our own pace,
Once we open a door of access to someone, an
association, friendship or romance can then begin,
And how wide we open up each door determines
how much we let each person in.

The doors that provide access to opportunities on
the other hand are a very mysterious beast,
Because usually it is a mystery what lies behind each
one and they can often render the least,
A knock must be given as we wait patiently in front
any door that is closed to our human form,
And sometimes it will be opened up to us before we
surrender to defeat and then start to move along.

CHUNKS OF GOODNESS

Due to our curiosity we may wish to approach and
open a multitude of doors,
But there are some things that we really must
remember that truly cannot be ignored,
We may wish to spark new relationships and seek
out the realization of our dreams,
But other people are not always kind and
considerate and not every opportunity is what it
seems.

Sometimes a door of access can protect us from
those who will only cause us misery and pain,
And at times the doors of opportunity we knock
upon are really just the same,
Sometimes an opportunity when offered can result
in a very painful cost,
And so, at times a door of opportunity that remains
closed to us is not really an actual loss.

Flights of Companionship: Love and Friendship

When a new day arrives and lands upon the runway
of your life,
The day may bring with it flights of love and
friendship that might take you by surprise,
The flights of companionship that you choose to
board and fly upon will determine where you go,
And some friendships and lovers can at times,
provide an ounce of comfort to your soul.

Once you have boarded any flights of
companionship that you decided to choose,
Your seat belt must then be tightly fastened as your
relationships you start to peruse,
Some flights may experience turbulence and fly
across a very rocky path,
But there is always an escape hatch, if you need to
leave a flight extremely fast.

A parachute can be very useful, if you find yourself
in desperate need,
So, do not be afraid to jump out of the plane, if the
flight is not going where you initially believed,
The luggage compartment of the plane is not a very
nice place to sit, live or be,
And so, if your friend or lover seats you there, it is
better to jump out and to be free.

CHUNKS OF GOODNESS

If you find yourself upon a flight that is filled with
nothing but pain and misery,
You may have to leave that flight and find another
journey that makes you truly happy,
Another flight may take a while to come along but
once it arrives as it waits for you to board,
You might find that flight suits your heart much
more and that your joy will then be fully restored.

Deportation of Pretenders

In the land of my life are some citizens that really
should not be there,
Because they bring me nothing but drama,
heartache, grief and despair,
These deceptive pretenders have caused me so
many painful tears,
Because they have manipulated my weaknesses and
capitalized upon my fears,
But deep down inside myself I now know the
decision that I must make,
Because all they do each day from my life is just
take, take and take,
So now they must be permanently deported from
my peaceful life, mind and heart,
Because they did not appreciate me right from the
very start.

Such a difficult decision can be so very hard to
actually see through,
But their presence in my life is not sincere and I
know that much is true,
Each day of life can be filled to the brim with lots of
pain or joy,
But the more I tolerate the pretenders, the longer I
will be their toy,
Every one of them I've granted a visa to will waste
my tears, years and time,
And so, I must always remember that it is not their

CHUNKS OF GOODNESS

life to colonize and that in fact, it's mine,
The bundles of delight that life can offer patiently
wait for me to be free,
But first I must deport the pretenders because the
space they occupy in my life is truly not meant to be.

The Enemy of Hatred

An enemy exists that resides inside each human
mind and heart,
His name is Hatred and in every mortal life he plays
his silent part,
Although Hatred seems to be quite quiet and even
at times very far away,
Rather mysteriously somehow, he is actually present
every day,
When we walk through storms of heartbreak or fall
into a pit of despair,
Although Hatred seems so far away, he can
suddenly, strangely appear,
Once you decide to release Hatred from your mind,
mouth, lips and tongue,
The battle for peace within you has only really just
begun,
Because Hatred can quickly start to possess your
mind, body and soul,
And once you belong to Hatred, he will then
attempt to fulfil his ugly goal.

Fortunately, some defensive weapons to conquer
Hatred do actually exist,
Because love and forgiveness are temptations that
he simply cannot resist,
A shield of patience can protect you from Hatred's
powerful attacks,
But be prepared for a war as determination is not

something that he lacks,
The battle with Hatred inside of you may continue
for many days and nights,
But eventually love will overcome his power and
then an end will be in sight,
Once Hatred grows tired and weary, your victory can
then be realized,
But do not let your guard down because Hatred is a
true master of disguise,
In just a matter of seconds, he can return and then
fully consume your mind,
Because Hatred has many access routes and your
weaknesses are easy for him to find.

The Life Nobody Wanted to Live In

In the library of life parked upon a solitary shelf,
There sits a lonely form that somehow ignores
himself,
A reluctant soul that shuns his human vessel
every single day,
With not a wish to participate in a human life in
any way,
Sadly, that human life is now no longer wanted
by any soul at all,
Because a lack of joy has been that human
vessel's tragic downfall,
No smiles, no tears, no laughter and not even any
doubts,
Emanate from that human form and there are no
joyful shouts,
That life really could not have been given to
anybody else,
And so, it remained redundant upon that lonely,
solitary shelf,
Unwanted, unloved, rejected, cast aside and
absolutely spurned,
As the years passed by very sadly, no lessons
were ever learned,
No wisdom was joyfully gathered or human
contributions made,
Because the owner of that human life did nothing
but hoped for his grave.

CHUNKS OF GOODNESS

A few passers-by at times did actually stop and
then start to stare,
But no one wanted to live in that life because it
was devoid of any social flair,
An ignored, abandoned life with very little human
essence or appeal,
They had no reason to want it as the years that
passed by did reveal,
And as the deserted, lonely human vessel
gradually started to age,
No change was forthcoming and so the Giver of
Life began to rage,
Why won't you live inside that human life, Giver
of Life demanded, I gave you so much,
Yet you sit here wrapped in solitary sadness with
your heart untouched,
Many questions were posed that day to the
reluctant soul,
As the Giver of Life tried desperately to find some
kind of sense to it all,
Finally, a response was offered as the soul began
to weep,
I am scared to live a human life and I am scared
to fall asleep,
Bravery eludes me, he explained, and I cannot do
it alone,
And there is no one there to comfort me at night
when I return to my home.

Decorate your life with gratitude, Giver of Life

advised,
And then someone may love you and you will not
be despised,
If you are pleasant, kind and compassionate to
those that you meet along the way,
Then people may want to be your friend which
will appease your mind and keep sadness at bay,
A smile suddenly crossed Giver of Life's face as
the lonely soul began to stand,
And then the two started to prepare for his soul
to return to the human, mortal land,
Life is not always pleasant, Giver of Life advised,
and that much I do know,
But truly it must be lived because ultimately that
is a soul's main goal,
Once a human life comes to an end, you will wish
that you had lived so much more,
Because unrealized wishes, hopes and dreams will
then remain forever unexplored,
Sometimes there will be ups and sometimes there
will be downs,
And there will be days filled with happiness and
days full of sad, tearful frowns,
But if you try to make your life joyful, you will
never truly be alone,
Because Happiness is a friend that will always
comfort you and warm the interior of your human
home.

Equilibrium of Peace

Inside my mind there is a set of shiny, golden
scales,
Which attempt to find a balance that will allow
peace to prevail,
Because peace is an essential component in the
machinery of life,
Which ensures that our objectives can be met
with minimum strife,
Like a lubricant that oils the engines of our
thoughts and mind,
Peace is a pleasant necessity that we must always
strive to find.

Although peace is intangible and has no physical
substance or shape,
Some pursue it to the ends of the Earth and give
their all for peace's sake,
Highly sought after, established and one that
commands silent respect,
Peace is the very essence of life that so many will
battle to protect,
A highly prized, invaluable treasure that is so
deeply revered,
Every day you that live a peaceful life is a day that
you have lived without any fear.

The scales inside my mind ensure that peace in
my life can frequently be found,
As I balance each factor carefully and measure

CHUNKS OF GOODNESS

each one pound for pound,
If anything disturbs the equilibrium of peace that
I enthusiastically seek,
I then try to find an appropriate solution quickly
because too much conflict can make you feel so
weak,
Every conflict that you engage in requires your
energy, your focus and your time,
And those who like to waste your life will think
that any unnecessary conflict that they cause is
absolutely fine.

What Do You See When You Look at Me?

What do you see when you look at me,
Our eyes are a window to our minds, thoughts
and hearts,
That explore visions of others and what we
perceive of them on our part,
The lenses of our perception look at people in so
many different ways,
Whilst we discover the wonders of the world
around us and those it contains.

So, what do you see when you look at me,
Because in every visual exchange there is your
perception of me and my perception of you,
But at times we must question if what we see in
others is really, actually true,
Inherently there can be so much hidden
underneath the human flesh, skin and form,
And sometimes our perceptive compass can form
misguided opinions of others that are truly wrong.

And so, what do you see when you look at me,
Because when I was homeless, looked unkempt,
rough and unwashed,
What would you see if you walked past me when
my home I had lost,
A dirty creature sat upon the stairs with no place
to call home and matted hair,

CHUNKS OF GOODNESS

But inside of me there really was so much more,
My potential which with some help, I had a
chance to explore.

And so, what do you see when you look at me,
Because when I was struck down with the
condition Guillain-Barre,
A wheelchair became my legs when I lost my
physical capacity and abilities,
What would you see if you met me when I could
not walk or run,
Just a wheelchair bound cripple or a human
being with a mind, heart and tongue.

Sometimes our perceptions of others can cripple
lives more than we realize,
And create more issues for people with unusual
challenges as they attempt to live decent lives,
Opportunities and access are an important
necessity that can allow human beings to achieve,
And negative attitudes can imprison and restrict
people, formed from what we may wrongly perceive,
So, if we open our thoughts, hearts and minds to
someone else's unfortunate circumstance,
We can set people free when we open up doors
of access to opportunities which might provide them
with a real chance.

Life Toolkit Tools

1. The Nation of Your Life
2. Decoration and Renovation of Your Life (Your Home)
3. Spring Clean of Life
4. The Garden of Our Hearts
5. The Kingdom of Your Life: Your Life, Your World, Your Kingdom
6. The Eyes of Love, Hate, Tolerance and Indifference
7. Weapons of Love, Truth, False Hope and Lies
8. Time is Our Friend and Our Foe
9. Seven Gifts of Love
10. The Life Lived, Unlived and Expected

The Nation of Your Life

The nation of your life is governed by your mind,
body and heart,
Because you are the designer, architect and ruler
of every single part,
From the government seats that you appoint to
some of those that you hold dear,
To the thrones inside your palace as your
personal monarchy you form and steer,
Your physical presentation and personal identity
represent your nation's flag,
Which at times you may fly at half mast, when
trouble blows your way and your mood starts to sag,
Your values, culture and beliefs are how you
govern your life and individual land,
As you live by your ethical standards and the
policies that you can both create and command.

Every part of your individual domain must be
kept in order and diligently maintained,
Because if your nation falls into disrepair then
your life may never be the same,
Just like any ruler, in your individual nation some
daily choices you must make,
Because you can decide those who visit you and
in your nation's splendour, partake and participate,
Each day will present you with challenges and
though you may make some mistakes,
A trip up the mountain of experience can assist
you and your land, restore and rejuvenate,

CHUNKS OF GOODNESS

A visit to the valley of wisdom will help you to
maintain your nation and help you to build your life,
So, try to visit those landmarks regularly, if you
want to do more than just survive.

Decoration and Renovation of Your Life (Your Home)

Every day that the sun dawns you have another
opportunity and chance,
To change the pace, appearance and tempo of your
life's joyful dance,
The interior of your human vessel that you always
live inside,
Can be decorated to provide a home in which you
can happily reside,
The human house of love you live inside belongs to
only you,
And it is built with bricks of dedicated love that are
always faithful, loyal and true,
Walls built from relationships filled with joy and
laughter can make your home a warm, friendly
place,
And interior furnishings that are pleasant can put a
smile upon your face,
Education can provide stable pieces of furniture that
will enhance your home,
And the solid structure of training can be a firm
foundation that does not ever roam.

Bright friendships can excite your mind, motivate
you and refresh your thoughts,
But to your life peaceful, consistent, stable
characters can also contribute a lot,
So, build and decorate your days and life with who

and what you wish to be near,
Because to some extent our lives can be defined by
our decisions that much is very clear,
Our relationships are like the walls of our life which
can provide comfort and stability,
And the appliances are the engines that represent
our careers and professionality,
Once your human home has been adorned with the
decor, furniture and appliances that you adore,
Then you may choose to indulge in some
experiences which like a cheerful song can
invigorate your core,
When the surroundings of your life have been fully
built and decorated as you truly desire and wish,
Your dance through life should then be much
brighter because your human home has been given
a transformative uplift.

Spring Clean of Life

The cobwebs in my mind may gather upon the
shelves of my thoughts like drops of painful dew,
But once a year I know for certain, there is
something that I must definitely do,
I must clear out all the cupboards inside my
thoughts filled with heartache, misery and pain,
And give the shelves of yesterday a thorough
dust because every inch of my life I have to
maintain.

The cupboards inside your mind may house many
painful cobwebs and even some layers of hurtful
dust,
And so, a regular clean out of your heart and
mind to eliminate any sorrow, really is a must,
A refreshment of your approach to life can
restore your heart and provide such a pleasant
change,
Because then a new song will fill up and lift your
heart once your life has been tidied up and
rearranged.

The Garden of Our Hearts

Inside the garden of my heart stands a sturdy oak
tree,
That illustrates to me clearly what love should
really be,
Strong, loyal, brave, steadfast, considerate and
kind,
It represents the kind of love that I need to give
and find,
When the rain of betrayal becomes heavy and
pours down from the skies,
The sturdy oak branches welcome and protect
me, so that I am not drenched by lies.

When I take a walk through the garden of love
that lives inside my heart,
I contemplate every lovable possibility as I
actively play my part,
Around the perimeter of my garden there sits a
silent, grey, steadfast stone wall,
To protect me from intruders and any strife which
may make me stumble and fall,
A wall of strength can protect you from what and
who should not be there,
Because that wall guards your heart daily from
any pretentious, deceptive snares.

Within the garden of your heart you may find
some very rough and rugged weeds,

But some flowers may still blossom from amongst
the scattered seeds,
Every flower of love that you plant will need
tender loving care,
Because love must be nurtured regularly and of
that reality you must truly be aware,
So, if you decide to venture into the garden of
love that lives deep inside of you,
Your path of participation must be chosen wisely
to find a real love that is sincere and true.

The Kingdom of Your Life: Your Life, Your World, Your Kingdom

Inside of you there is a kingdom that much is
very true,
Which governs how you live your life and
everything that you do,
But the politics of your mind and heart are really
not alone,
Because reason and logic sit thoughtfully upon
their respective thrones.

All of the emotions inside of you that you feel
every day,
Fight for control daily as your actions each one
may try to sway,
Your environment that surrounds you is part of
your domain,
As you attempt to govern your life, body and
heart with your solitary brain.

Your land and kingdom will remain unconquered
until love makes a start,
And you decide to give someone else the
precious keys to your treasured heart,
So be wary of the power that you give to those
you love so true,
Because they can make you suffer, inflict pain and
misery and make you feel so blue.

CHUNKS OF GOODNESS

If your kingdom is savaged or invaded and then
torn to shreds,
You will have to rebuild it with many delicate
threads,
The threads of wisdom can help you to recreate
the tapestry of your life,
And the needles of experience can pierce through
any obstacles of strife.

Always try to govern your kingdom wisely so that
you can avoid a war,
With those who cross your path mischievously or
take advantage from afar,
A mortal human being has only one actual mind,
heart and life to give,
But each new day is another chance for you to
rule the kingdom in which you live.
The threads of wisdom can help to recreate the
tapestry of your life,
And the needles of experience can pierce through
any obstacles of strife.

The Eyes of Love, Hate, Tolerance and Indifference

Although my face is a home to two physical eyes,
Really, I have eight because my inner thoughts
the two disguise,
Four sets of eyes and ways to look at the world
that I see,
And four ways to view life and the people that
surround me.

First of all, there is my most precious look of love
that I save for those I adore,
Which views them as if they have been sent from
heaven above as some of their imperfections I may
ignore,
Each time I glance at them my perception is true,
sincere and pure,
Because I appreciate their personas with a
softness that endures.

The second set of eyes I have which is really not
the same,
Is kept for those I tolerate that irritate my
thoughts like drops of rain,
I look at them so differently because I see them
through a very dreary lens,
Since they are not my confidants, companions or
even regarded as my friends.

CHUNKS OF GOODNESS

Another look I have which belongs to a different
train of thought,
Is the look of indifference for those I really do not
support,
The way I look at those that I feel totally
indifferent about,
Means that they have no emotional investment
from my love account.

Last but not least, I have a final set of very hateful
eyes,
That abhors every inch of those that hurt me,
who I really do despise,
When I look at someone in that hateful, angry,
bitter, resentful way,
I will never pay heed to anything that they do, or
listen to a single word they say.

Along with my emotions which in some I choose
to invest,
I only give my look of love to those who pass the
test,
Since I cannot afford to give away love that will
never be returned,
Because life is really too precious to spend each
day rejected, unloved and spurned.

Weapons of Truth, Love, False Hope and Lies

An armoury lies hidden inside each person's mind,
body and heart,
With accessible weapons at our disposal which
silently play their part,
Some weapons can create pleasure and some inflict
wounds and pain,
But all can be utilized to injure another person's
heart, mind and human frame.

The first weapon that stands silently and boldly, tall
upon the shelf,
Is the courageous sword of truth that it seems, likes
to remain by itself,
Strong, powerful, brave, righteous and sharp it
sparkles every day like new,
With a blade that can cut through ropes of lies,
when someone ties their deception around you.

Another dangerous weapon which sits in a quiet
corner, alone upon the ground,
Is the club of lies which inside every human armoury
can easily be found,
People often fear the profound damage that the
club of lies can inflict,
Because many people use it to manipulate what
other people believe and think.
The deadliest weapon inside the armoury sits alone

inside a protective ribcage,
Because the bomb of love can destroy everything
nearby when in a deadly rage,
If the bomb of love is detonated, it can explode in so
many destructive ways,
And destroy lives, hearts and people because love
contains death in its explosive rays.

Some other weapons include the ropes of false
promises and the fog of false hope that blinds,
Because when you tie the ropes of false promises
around someone else's life you can create a tricky
knot that binds,
The fog of false hope can blind and deceive people
and can ultimately destroy their lives,
As they wait for fake miracles to materialize that are
nothing but a bunch and pack of lies.

Some of these weapons can also be utilized as a
powerful method of defence,
Because truth and love can equip you when you face
a battle against pretence,
But one thing you must always remember, if
someone uses the weapon of false hope to attack
you,
Your own weapon of love may then work against
you because love can obscure what is really true.

Time is Our Friend and Our Foe

I have a very unusual friend that silently walks
through life with me,
His name is Time and sometimes, he is not what he
appears to be,
At times he can be so kind but at other times, he can
be so very harsh,
Because sometimes he assists me and at other times
our agendas seem to clash.

For Time only one thing truly, really matters because
he only has one role to play,
To ensure that each second ticks by as it should
because that is the objective of his day,
Regardless of what I do or don't do with each
minute, to Time it is non sequitur,
As he continues to walk along his path because each
second's passing he must secure.

Sometimes it almost seems as if Time slips away oh
so very fast,
As he strides across the face of the Earth and follows
his predetermined path,
But at other times Time seems to slowly crawl along
the ground of my day just like a snail,
Usually when I have tedious or difficult tasks to
complete, most of which I am likely to fail.

When Procrastination decides to pay my mind a

CHUNKS OF GOODNESS

visit, Time then rapidly becomes my foe,
As my mind quickly becomes distracted and I lose
sight of my overall goal,
The day can then become a tangled mess as
Procrastination leads me astray,
Because Procrastination does not like Time and so
provokes him in every imaginable way.

At times I wish I could speak to Time and ask him to
give me a longer day,
But Time is always too busy as his seconds, minutes
and hours silently tick away,
Every minute, hour, day and week for Time must
pass by as it should and must,
And Time has truly taught me that his delivery of my
years is something that I can always trust.

Each breath that Time takes every day is a second
that is released,
Which is then no longer accessible as every lived-out
moment rapidly becomes deceased,
When the minutes silently evaporate and as the
hours quietly disappear,
You will never see any of them again and of that
fact, Time is very clear.

Regardless of all Time's faults, there is one thing of
which you can truly be very sure,
Each day, month and year will continue whether you
give up on life, or choose to endure,

CHUNKS OF GOODNESS

Time can never change himself and so fixed and
constant he will forever remain,
Because the duration of every second, minute, hour
and day will always be the same.

Seven Gifts of Love

Seven gifts and ways to love someone live inside
our minds, hearts and human form,
And essentially although they are all very
different, they can be equally as strong,
Each one determines what we give of ourselves
to those that live inside our hearts, lives and world,
Because although love is intangible, it can steer
the ship of our heart through life's rocky perils,
Every single one is a different expression from
our hearts that symbolizes our human capacity,
As we love the world and people around us in
many different ways that suit our natural
propensities.

Agape is an innocent form of unconditional love
that exists inside our hearts,
And an undemanding gift of love for the family of
mankind of which we form a part,
Universal, idealistic and altruistic in kind, its
compassion can provoke us to care about humanity,
With this expression of love by our hearts to
those unknown to us which requires no familiarity,
Sacrificial compassionate acts towards others are
given with no agendas, demands or goals,
When we display expressions of agape love
because this love is described as the love of the soul.

Storge is a natural instinctive gift of love given to

those that we consider to be our family,
Our children, siblings, parents and those we
adopt into our lives and treat like royalty,
Engraved inside our hearts and given
unconditionally, dutifully and without expectations
or demands,
No objective or goal underlies this form of pure
love which is given through our hearts, hugs and
hands,
The gifts of supportive sacrificial provisions that
we give to our relatives, family and blood,
We provide whilst we stand through life beside
them with our loyal, steadfast, familial love.

Philia is an authentic, mutual kind of love that we
give willingly to our friends and associates,
That we see as our symmetric equals either in
character or another form, way or shape,
Unlike the seductive lure of Eros this type of love
is not governed by passionate, intimate desires,
Because Philia is a love that guides our hearts
with innocence not through lustful flames or erotic,
impulsive fires,
We may provide a shoulder to cry on, hopeful
encouragement, a crutch of support or even chunks
of hearty advice,
To those we consider our allies in life as we
attempt to navigate our way through the rocky
mountains of our lives.

Eros is the manifestation of the flames of passion
that ignite our desires and the pursuit of internal
lusts,
But Eros can take us on a ride of heartbreak
because he can steer us towards rocks of deceit and
mistrust,
Unlike Agape and Philia, Eros only cares about
the fulfillment of his own objectives in his world,
As he hides inside our hearts and minds and
provokes us to maximize our passionate whirls,
If we allow Eros to rule us, a life of unfulfilled
passion and unrequited love we may then endure,
Because Eros can be a poor master that cares
very little about our long term needs of that I am
very sure.

Pragma is the epitome and long-term
commitment of the convenient gift of self,
To a relationship that may suit certain life goals
and render various forms of economic wealth,
Practical, dutiful, expectant, conditional, business
like and with a goal congruent utility core,
This type of because love is based on what one
can give and receive from any relationship explored,
A shared common goal can be worked towards, if
an attitude of mutual reciprocation does exist,
But pragma is not a truly idealistic gift to give
because it involves love with a materialistic, tradable
twist.

CHUNKS OF GOODNESS

Ludus is a gift of love that is playful which is
given predominantly for casual fun,
That comprises of the pursuit of intimate sporty
conquests that require more than one,
Usually associated with lovers, competitive rivals
and playful friendships of a very flirtatious kind,
This type of love lacks commitment and is not
one that is meaningful or that truly binds,
Although sometimes ludus can develop into
something much more long-term and even more
sincere,
Initially, this love is based on teasing, pranks and
pleasure but intentions are not always clear.

Philautia is the self-indulgent gift of love that you
will at times give to yourself,
Because an investment into your own life will
never be wasted or placed upon a pretentious shelf,
Self-love is a necessary safety net that we must
give ourselves a portion of each day,
Because an empty vessel, mind and heart cannot
satisfy ourselves or others in any single way,
The way in which we love ourselves depends on
how much we value who we are and who we aspire
to become,
And so, if we wish to reside in happiness a
regular, internal performance review of our interior
must definitely be done.

The Life Lived, Unlived and Expected

Some people talk about their human life as if there
really is only one,
Yet strangely, I have realized, there is a lot more to
this life that we live under the earthly Sun,
Each person that lives a human life does not just
have one life that they choose to live,
They also have the life that they could have lived to
which time they did not devote and give,
Every choice that you make becomes the life in
which you choose to participate,
And the dormant opportunities that lie behind you
were another route that you had a chance to take,
Another life lies directly in front of us and that is the
life that we expect to materialize,
But that depends upon the plans we place our trust
in that may or may not be realized,
Each second of our life becomes our choice which
then determines all three,
As we live the life lived, unlived and expected and
choose who we wish to be.

Life Choices and Emotional Survival Tools

11. Right Choice, Wrong Moment! Right Moment, Wrong Choice!
12. Hope: Drug of Comfort and a Dinner of Deceit
13. Labyrinth of Despair
14. The Doormat
15. Hidden Sanctuary of Your Thoughts
16. Quality Control
17. Snakes, Ladders and Puppy-dog Tails
18. The Storm of Heartbreak
19. Teardrops of Healing Comfort
20. Goodbye is Not Forever

Right Choice, Wrong Moment! Right Moment, Wrong Choice!

A maze of choices lies before us as in life we try
to find our path and way,
Because for our actual life there is no manual that
we can read and apply every day,
Each choice we face and make is an opportunity
that will have a hidden cost,
Because other opportunities we then forsake and
other outcomes are then lost.

Our individual life choices can be a very complex,
intricate and personal affair,
Because there are so many factors that may
provoke us to follow a path somewhere,
Some of those factors are not something that we
can always predict, control or gauge,
Because our access to information is not perfect
so that can be a major disadvantage.

There are many different types of decisions that
we may often decide to make,
That depend upon our own internal preferences
and even our emotional state,
At times we may make a choice based upon our
situation and our personal circumstance,
And sometimes we might make a decision naively
and be led upon a very deceptive dance.

CHUNKS OF GOODNESS

Predictable choices when offered are usually,
immediately snapped up,
Because a particular option instantly appeals to
us and so we may feel that we are in luck,
Due to the fact that our individual preferences
may lean a certain way,
When faced with such a decision, foreseeability
quickly comes into play.

Dictated decisions are a very different beast
formed from heavy arms of steel,
Which determine what we choose in life, no
matter what we think or how we feel,
This kind of choice presents itself to us in
disguise and is not actually a real choice at all,
Because various factors put pressure upon us to
follow someone else's protocols.

Reactionary decisions are another very different
type of choice,
That occur when we respond to something else
that has happened in our lives,
Our reaction and response may be impulsive,
negative and even immediate,
As we subsequently react to what others do and
try to defend or retaliate.

Informed choices and decisions are something
very rare and are really quite unique,
Because to have access to all the relevant

information to accurately make a choice is a
perfection that we often seek,
Such decisions are usually much wiser and more
carefully thought through,
Because facts and knowledge are trusted guides
that can enlighten us and determine what we do.

Uninformed choices and decisions are generally,
a negative, ambiguous crowd to meet,
Which can often result in chaos, havoc and
destruction that can knock us of our feet,
A lack of wisdom and errors of judgement can
often infiltrate our minds and then silently start to
reign,
Because the information that we require to make
a good choice is not fully visible to our brains.

Instinctive choices and decisions that we make
come from deep inside,
That may be formed by our own individual
preferences, leanings and foresight,
These can often be shaped by experiences that
we have been through in the past,
As we try to utilize hindsight to steer our boat of
life and to provide a knowledgeable mast.

Emotional decisions are usually the most
irrational choices that we will ever make,
As we allow our feelings to determine the choices
that we should select and which to forsake,

CHUNKS OF GOODNESS

Sometimes fear can dictate our choices as we try
to avoid a negative repetition of events,
And often our decisions are steered by those we
hold dear to us, according to our inner sentiments.

Circumstantial decisions depend upon our
personal situation, lifestyle and circumstance,
Which can be influenced by our finances, social
bonds and our status in terms of romance,
Everything that surrounds us inside the
environment of our lives and world with which we
associate,
Can have a direct impact upon what we choose
as the terms of our existence, we seek to negotiate.

Another consideration lies silently before us when
we face a choice and a crossroads,
And that is the moment of its arrival which is a
crucial factor that cannot be ignored,
Some choices may be right for us but better for
our lives at another point in time,
If we wish to ensure that our overall objectives in
life and decisions fully align.

Once our decisions have been made each day,
another problem may then have to be faced,
Because the right moment may have been
present but we chose the wrong option and made a
mistake,
Right moments and wrong choices are not an

ideal coupling that really get along,
And a marriage between the two will never truly
be happy, blissful or very strong.

Peace within our minds and hearts can at times
be reached to some extent,
If we try to make our choices wisely and
thoughtfully to avoid any regrets or discontent,
Once a decision has been implemented, we will
then have to live with the subsequent
responsibilities,
So, it is essential that we understand the choices
that we face so that we can make our decisions
carefully.

Hope: Drug of Comfort and Dinner of Deceit

Like a drug that pacifies the portion of hope that I
had consumed temporarily comforted my mind,
But doubts suddenly began to surface because
solutions in reality I could not find,
I had bought into the dream of a better
tomorrow as I had sacrificed a truly awful today,
But the meal of hopeful wishes that I had eaten
could not sustain me and so the threads of hope
began to fray,
And as I stood in front of the dumpster of my life
filled with my broken heart and dreams,
I then began to quietly consider the reality of
what hope actually represents and means,
Hope can joyfully be evoked by promises,
thoughts, visions, dreams and plans,
But hope can also lead to our downfall when trust
is placed in the wrong hands,
A tricky dinner of deceit that can be prepared for
us by those that we appreciate,
To exploit positions of power as our lives they
sabotage, take for granted and deceptively try to
break,
The only hope you can truly trust in is a hope that
emanates from within yourself,
Because some people try to use hope as a snare
to destroy your life as they plot your downfall in
stealth.

Labyrinth of Despair

A tragedy suddenly struck the heart of my life
and my life I could not resume,
As I rapidly slipped down into the labyrinth of
despair and was silently consumed,
Grief and sadness suddenly gripped my heart as I
was engulfed in distress,
But my mind still tried to make sense of it all to
see if the pain hurt any less,
Every pore of my flesh began to weep and exude
a nervous, fearful sweat,
As I frantically searched for an exit from that
maze of painful hurt and tearful regrets,
Unfortunately, no exit seemed to appear and no
solutions could be found,
And as the weeks went by, my heart remained
torn apart as it lay crushed upon the ground,
No map was ever provided and no light was
shone upon my path to guide me through,
And so, I wandered aimlessly through the
labyrinth's dark tunnels, uncertain what to do.

Sadly, I finally began to conclude that my life
could not be fully restored,
As I started to accept that despair had buried me
deep inside its core,
A rescue would not happen and no hero it
seemed would ever really appear,
Because all that surrounded me now was

negativity, pain and hurt, sadness, tears and fear,
Suddenly however, it dawned upon me that there
was truly, only one real way out,
As I began to inspect the passageways of my
thoughts and dissect my incessant doubts,
My heart and mind had to face, accept and cope
with the tragedy that had taken place,
Because my life had been attacked by a whirlwind
of destruction that had no actual face,
The nurse of Time would have to take my hand
and heal me and then guide me back to my own life,
So that slowly I would start to live again because
an exit from the maze of pain, Time would gradually
provide.

The Doormat

The hallway of life for me was once a very
optimistic, pleasant, joyful place,
But one day that suddenly changed as misery
stepped in and showed its ugly face,
Dark shadows from the past I quickly realized,
now obstructed every single door,
And the hopeful, pleasant life that I had once
lived, was enjoyable no more,
Each door of access to opportunities had
somehow been obstructed and fully blocked,
By the shadows of misery from yesterday that
now haunted my life as they taunted me and
mocked,
Although their shadows hung over me, I tried to
carry on with my walk-through life,
But I already knew what they could do to me and
all about their miserable strife.

Every step I took was very painful as I bravely
tried to approach each door,
But the shadows quickly knocked me down to the
ground and so I ended up strewn across the floor,
My being then became their doormat as they
tormented and taunted me each day,
And as they wiped their feet upon my face in
every imaginable, callous way,
Bitterness rapidly became the only friend I had
that actually remained,

CHUNKS OF GOODNESS

Because every drop of joy had been squeezed
out of my life and happiness forgot my name,
But the shadows heartless, iron rule over my life
was not yet actually done,
Because as I sadly discovered, they had not yet
exploited every part of me and they had only just
begun.

My life rapidly became their tool of misery with
which they could cruelly play,
As they rejoiced in every minute of heartbreak
and pain that they caused me and I could not say,
No one understood the pain I had suffered, or
the trauma that I had lived through,
Because their form of exploitation was different
and not something many people recognize or do,
Each time my life crumbled as they forced me to
live in a land of emotional distress,
I would just pick up the pieces of my broken life
and try to sort out the disgusting mess,
They often rejoiced heartlessly in the pain that
they had caused me as they reaped every possible
reward,
And the years of my life that they had stolen from
me was denied, disregarded and ignored.

A domestic skivvy and colonized slave for
decades, my life had been totally ransacked,
As I searched desperately for a ladder of support
to escape from their hellish traps and attacks,

CHUNKS OF GOODNESS

The land of decency was a beautiful place and it
was where I had happily once lived,
But I had been trampled into their gutter of
abuse for so very long and so now, I could no longer
forgive,
Torn down, destroyed, exploited and abused in
every possible manner and form,
They had made my life a total hellhole as they
had unleashed their abusive, predatory storms,
Every miserable day I tried to stay away from
them but they would not stop or cease,
And as they stood upon my head and inflicted
wounds of painful misery, I could find no peace.

I had done my best to hide from them, avoided
them and even asked them to stop,
But they would not let me exist in peace without
their abusive, predatory onslaught,
Every day I breathed and lived, I hoped and
wished that they would go away,
Yet they were never satisfied because upon my
life they relentlessly continued to prey,
When my broken heart was in shattered
fragments and as I tried to stand up once more,
I began to pick up the remnants of my stolen life
as I observed their predatory encore,
Once their reign of abusive exploitation finally
finished and came to an actual end,
I then began to tearfully rebuild my life alone
with bricks of love as I became my own best friend.

Hidden Sanctuary of Your Thoughts

Inside your mind there lives a very special place,
Which in your moments of trial you can fully
embrace,
A hidden secret part of you that no one else can
see,
It gives you the liberty and luxury to be truly free.

When the world attacks you and it seems nobody
really cares,
In that special place you can find solace without
any hateful stares,
Private, quiet, peaceful, gentle, caring, serene and
kind,
That special pleasant place exists only inside your
own mind.

A blanket of warmth it can shelter you from life's
many storms,
And comfort you when the human fabric of your
life has been torn,
It is a secret place that no one else can enter
because it cannot be seen,
And within it you can hide your truths, desires,
wishes, hopes and dreams.

Access to your thoughts can be given to only
those who you permit,
Because your mind is a hidden sanctuary with a

very peaceful remit,
Although angry attitudes and hateful words may
attack you from all sides,
Inside your mind there is always a loving place for
you to hide and reside.

At times your life can be ripped to shreds and
you may fall apart,
But a safe hiding place always exists inside your
mind, body and heart,
Be strong and find that peaceful place when the
world becomes cold and rough,
Because that inner sanctuary of love will warm
you and provide shelter when life is harsh and
tough.

Quality Control

Deep inside the passageways of my mind, a
quality control conveyor belt can be found,
Which checks the quality of my connections to
ensure that my relationships are truly sound,
Those that fail to meet the standards of respect
that I have established and maintained,
Are then politely rejected because a code of
decency must be adhered to and sustained.

Throughout every aspect of my life I reserve the
right to exist and live,
Without the needles of discomfort caused by any
heartache that others may try to give,
A process of elimination is the only way to ensure
that my expectations will be met,
Because associates, friends and lovers should be
your allies in life and not an actual threat.

Definition is essential element when a new
relationship starts to take on an actual form,
Because you must identify what behaviour is
appropriate and which interactions truly belong,
Undefined relationships can often become quite
murky and rapidly gather stress,
Because muddled interactions can easily slip into
an ambiguous, chaotic, hectic mess.

Measurement is another tool that can be utilized

from the toolkit inside your mind,
Because prickly and tricky associates, friends and
lovers will never be truly kind,
Once you have compared your interactions to the
standards of respect that you create and set,
Then you can approve of any new relationships, if
your code of decency has been fully met.

Analysis is imperative if you want the course of
your relationships to be smooth,
As you seek to eliminate any issues that may
potentially disrupt the associations that you choose,
Any problematic areas in your relationships
should be identified so that you can peacefully
proceed,
Because a turbulent, rocky, stormy relationship is
a distraction that you really don't want or need.

Improvement is always possible, if you feel that a
relationship is not quite up to scratch,
But if too much improvement is required, a
connection should be assigned to the defect batch,
If a negative relationship is deemed to be worth
more effort because to a person you are deeply
attached,
Then you must embark upon some construction
work to build, improve and renovate every rocky
patch.

Control is the last mechanism that can help you

to manage your personal and professional affairs,
As you attempt to make the environment of your
life a joyful one without any hateful snares,
If you control how you interact with others and
decide how much of your life you want to share,
You can maximize the quality of your life with
quality relationships that should be constructive,
positive and fair.

Snakes, Ladders and Puppy-dog Tails

In this game of life there are some very complex
affairs,
Because we may find some snakes that slither
that can catch us unaware,
Ladders of opportunity can help us reach a very
great height,
But slippery snakes will try to drag us down with
all of their might.

Sometimes ladders may present themselves to us
but we might fail to see,
Opportunities that we can pursue as we follow
our chosen paths quite ignorantly,
Some ladders that we may find can be very tricky
and are not meant to be climbed by us at all,
Because to do so might hurt somebody that we
love and could usher in our downfall.

Some other ladders are always present but those
lie silently inside our own minds,
And these are the ladders of virtue which
determine whether we are harsh or kind,
Each one can form a constructive part of how we
live our lives every single day,
Because our choices and decisions are governed
by the things we think, do and say.

Slippery snakes of betrayal can hide along the

CHUNKS OF GOODNESS

paths that we choose to walk along in life,
And if they pounce upon us unexpectedly, they
can cause us heartache, calamity and strife,
To avoid those snakes is virtually impossible
because they can suddenly appear anywhere,
But if we surround ourselves with decency then
we give them less of a chance to build a hateful
snare.

Another type of snakes exist that lie in wait for us
inside our own core,
Which are our own vices that can ultimately
demolish us and destroy our lives even more,
If we allow our negative vices to govern our lives
and those we love, we betray and forsake,
We may steer our ship of life into the rocks of
doom and create a shipwreck of heartbreak.

Inside the jungle of life's choices, one supportive
consolation may exist,
The puppy-dog tails of love and care offered to
us by those in our midst,
Advice and support from those who care about
us can stop us from falling off a destructive cliff,
Because a puppy-dog tail of loving consideration
can be a lifeline that we should not simply dismiss.

A puppy-dog tail of support can be a stiff
disapproval that may warn, or a happy joyful swing,
As those who love us offer opinions, wisdom and

advice that can potentially enlighten,
Whether we accept a puppy-dog tail offering of
advice is another choice that we must then make,
But we must always remember that some
relationships are very artificial and are really fake.

Just like snakes and ladders, puppy-dog tails can
have more than one side,
Because if there is an ulterior motive behind
someone else's support, we might be taken for a
ride,
So, when we embark upon our walk-through life
each day we have to thoughtfully prepare,
For any snakes and ladders that may be scattered
across our path and let wisdom guide us into the
right thoroughfare.

Storm of Heartbreak

A storm of heartbreak suddenly hit my boat of
life one day and it began to rock from side to side,
And with the jagged rocks of destruction and
despair, my human vessel then threatened to collide,
The storm had hit my life very rapidly with no
warning signs and so I was not prepared,
When heartbreak and misery threatened to
destroy everything about which I truly cared.

The relentless storm started to wreak havoc upon
every single part of my life,
As a whirlwind of destruction cut away at my life
frantically just like a sharp knife,
When my life had been viciously ripped to shreds
and I could stand up no more,
Then I finally had to accept that the storm of
heartbreak and misery could no longer be ignored.

Every single part of my life had been totally and
utterly, completely destroyed,
But deep down I knew that I would have to repair
and fix it as the stormy attack started to subside,
No one else would reconstruct my life and pick
up all the debris of hurt and pain,
And no one else was going to heal my heart and
put the broken pieces back together again.

Although I could no longer stand up tall or hold

CHUNKS OF GOODNESS

my head up to the sky,
Because the storm had crushed every single part
of my life, a reality I cannot deny,
I bravely crawled along the ground as I began to
collect the remnants of yesterday,
Because fortunately, the storm that had rocked
my ship of life had not been there to stay.

One thing suddenly struck me as I knelt up and
then started to slowly rebuild my world,
To fix my life would take much longer than the
storm's attack which had destroyed it in a whirl,
The devastation that had been caused and the
horrific damage that had been done,
Had taken place in a blink of an eye as the storm
had unleashed its destructive guns.

Sometimes a frustrated part of me wanted to give
up and not repair my life at all,
And at times I had to push myself to carry on as
mockers rejoiced at my fall,
Those who had heartlessly destroyed me would
not fix the mess that they had made,
And so, I would have to rebuild my life with bricks
of love alone because it is my life to the grave.

Heartbreak to an individual life can be like an
unexpected, destructive storm,
And those who usually cause it, once the storm
subsides, vanish and are gone,

So, the storms of life must first be weathered and
then the broken pieces of your life must be picked
up by you,
Because the agents of heartbreak and misery
usually just leave behind, the painful debris of what
they do.

Teardrops of Healing Comfort

Despair and tragedy came to visit me one day
and their company I could not avoid,
And as I ran straight into the rocks of heartbreak
and destruction, my boat of life did suddenly
capsize,
Misery washed over, swallowed and engulfed me
as I was dragged down into the murky depths of
despair and pain,
And no joy or sunshine could be found as I was
rapidly buried under a mountain of disdain,
No ladder of hope was provided to help me
clamber out and escape from the pit of misery,
So, for a while I wallowed in my own pain which
seemed to have no solution or remedy,
But as my tears started to flow down my cheeks
and my sadness was finally released,
Each teardrop seemed to clean the internal
wounds that hurt me and the pain began to cease,
Every teardrop of comfort that I cried was like an
antiseptic to my emotional distress,
And as my wounds were cleansed internally, I
learnt to stand up again so that I could start to cope
with all the mess.

Goodbye is Not Forever

Goodbye is not forever, somebody once said to
me,
But now it seems as if our last goodbye really was
because your face I no longer see,
The tears I cry cannot express what you meant to
us all,
Because one day you just departed without a final
goodbye or a call,
Although my sadness cannot bring you back or
give you another day,
I hope that you have found a peaceful place to
rest now where you can finally stay.

Your soul departed way too soon and I really wish
you could still be here,
Because your hand and smile were a comfort to
me that I loved to be near,
There are things I should have said to you and
things we should have done,
But the train of regrets I sit on now, really cannot
be undone,
Though my life must continue now without you
by my side,
A part of me left with you, from that fact I cannot
hide.

Every part of me will always remember you the
way that you were as we wandered through life's

miles,
Because love does not just vanish from our hearts
into thin air despite life's many trials,
My heart and mind still want to keep your
memory alive,
Because through the rocky terrain of life, you
always stood by my side,
And although there is no return ticket to your
human abode,
I truly hope that you have found peace now
inside your beautiful soul.

Memories of our yesterdays formed from tears of
sadness are now really all that remain,
As I try to carry on with life without you and
silently shoulder the pain,
Although all our tomorrows must be forgotten
now because you are here no more,
One day I hope to see you again when I step
through heaven's door,
Every day I think about you even though we are
now physically apart,
Because you still live within me, inside my mind
and heart.

Thank you for purchasing this poetry collection.
Please have a good day and don't forget to smile, fine tune your thoughts and to put on your clothes of confidence.

www.ingramcontent.com/pod-product-compliance
Lightning Source LLC
Chambersburg PA
CBHW060516030426
42337CB00015B/1907